Lucy
Uncatalogued

Lucy Uncatalogued

Poems by

John Moody

© 2025 John Moody. All rights reserved.
This material may not be reproduced in any form, published,
reprinted, recorded, performed, broadcast,
rewritten, or redistributed without
the explicit permission of John Moody.
All such actions are strictly prohibited by law.

Cover design by Shay Culligan
Cover art by John Moody
Author photo by John Moody

ISBN: 978-1-63980-737-6
Library of Congress Control Number: 2025937562

Kelsay Books
502 South 1040 East, A-119
American Fork, Utah 84003
Kelsaybooks.com

The cover image is from a drawing of a photograph by David Brill of an Australopithecus skull reproduced on p.128 of the book co-written by Donald Johanson, called *From Lucy to Language*. These skulls, the center of that being's identity in life, often require painstaking reconstruction; a process that can never reconstruct the personality. That inventiveness requires the imagination.

for my wife Mary,
who endured months of hearing these poems read aloud

Acknowledgments

I acknowledge the editors of the following publications in which these poems first appeared sometimes in different versions:

Dreich: "Lucy Grieves," "Lucy's Legacy," "Lucy Reflects on Fame"
Writer's Umbrella: "Prediction"

Gratitude

I acknowledge the work of paleoanthropologist Dr Donald Johanson, Lucy's rediscoverer. His difficult and sometimes dangerous work provides an impetus for this collection.

For the drawings, I am indebted to the photographs of David Brill.

Poet Heidi Williamson and fellow printmaker Andrea Cardow. These were invaluable in allowing me to consider my position as an older male, assuming to voice a female perspective.

Fellow poets Stephen Eric Smyth, whose exhaustive critique helped shape these poems and Marc Sherland for his editing expertise.

My thanks go to Karen Kelsay and her team, who had faith in my first poetry pamphlet.

Some incidents in this poem sequence are based on events described in books written or co-authored by Dr Johanson. I interpret and embellish these events with views and comments that do not always reflect Dr Johanson's. The creative interpretation of the facts of Lucy's discovery and the subsequent fate of her remains are my own.

Contents

I Antecede You	17
The Hominid Family Tree	18
Lucy Recovered	19
The Naming of Fossils	21
Lucy as Medusa	22
Lucy Ruminates on Evolution	23
Huddle Besieged	24
Lucy Spurns Bondage	25
Lucy on History's Bones	27
Lucy's Glitz	28
Lucy's a Debutante	29
Lucy's Diamond Debut	30
The Knee Joint	31
Lucy Doin' the Loco-Motion	32
Lucy Reflects on Fame	33
Lucy Worshipped	34
Lucy's Exile	35
Dinkinesh	36
Join Me in Deep Time	38
Lucy as Lucifer	39
Lucy and Lucifer	40
You're Capering Urban Grasslands	41
Lucy and the Neanderthal	42
Peking Man	43
Homo Ergaster	44
Mrs Ples Provokes Hominid Fever	45
Who's on Lucy's Team?	46
Look Up Man	47
Prediction	48
Lucy Laid Out	49
Advance to Dim Futures	50
Lucy Grieves	51

The Sediments of Time	52
Lucy Fossilised Past-Future	53
I'm Lucy, No Wise Man	55
Entombed	56
Becoming Like Lucy	57
Notes	59

We name our thoughts, our paintings, but think to name a lake.

—Lorine Niedecker, notes made about her poem "Lake Superior"

*. . . We suffer from the delusion that the entire universe
is held in order by the categories of human thought,
fearing that if we do not hold to them with the utmost tenacity,
everything will vanish into chaos.*

—Alan Watts, *The Wisdom of Insecurity*

I Antecede You

stalking sapiens.
I was content as an early hominid,
now a rock-lump used to test your postulates.
I am a twig on the tree of your ancestry,
where my magical bones hang in your time.

The Hominid Family Tree

I'm Lucy   never oblivious   to

the hominid family tree.
As a spiky sapling, more stunted bush
than   arboreal effort,
     shrunk in its drawing
            and growing and I lie near the roots.
A hominid,
       a bough bent to the side
of its pullulation.
A dead-end for shoots   shrivelled
sunk in the fossil mud of my beginning.
     I'll wonder
if you'll outgrow poisoning your family tree?

Lucy Recovered

Every object of desire is a found object, traditionally at least.
—William Gibson

recovering fossil hom
inid remains is inhere
ntly destructive—
the fossil is plucked
from the
ground or ex
cavated
from
an
ancient
stratum
the speci
men is no
longer in its
original con
text and
some inform
ation is lost

He queries
the rarity of
my skull slivers

found
objects of
his desire

but he can never
truly know the truth of
my barren remains
when he's crawling Hadar
outcrops obsessively probing the st
one matrix, caressing me with dental
picks and brushes, probing my scarcity for
the narrative of my species before I erode into oblivion

I seek an oblivious act into my own oblivion

The Naming of Fossils

Naming fossils is no semantic matter,
for this bone collecting trendsetter.
One he can't mansplain in off-duty games.
Like a cat a fossil has three different names.
Firstly, a number of where she was found
tagging geolocation in hot arid ground.
Caress her with brushes, poke her with chisels.
Write her up in PALEO journals.
Then there's her scientific name
to proclaim his scholarly fame.
A name he announces in astute
arenas, slick in his blue safari suit.
Names that may end in afarensis,
neanderthalensis, even floresiensis.
Or six syllable Australopithecus;
count 'em—Aus tra lo pith e cus—
it's a name he invents to impress us.
But the name no human ever discovers,
Is the name a fossil had from her mother
Profound meditation, contemplation
of 'other,' never measures my fame
my fossil's ineffable, original name.

Patina
polished from
my fossil like
caries from my teeth
with my name
an old possum
gnawing into its burrow.

Lucy as Medusa

A Medusa-like trick,   I petrify,
stone shards scattered,
substance leached
into rock.
Molecules drowning
in coolly trickling mineral water.

No   horror-film flash:

sedately,
silently,
I wait.

Ossified over epochs
for my unveiling in the fierce,
evolving Ethiopian Hadar.

Lucy Ruminates on Evolution

I cannot join your world, but . . .

evolve with hope   sapiens.

You are the last human herd grazing.
My name forces me to your

side. Together we're . . . taking the knee,   but
never into our
self-domestication.
We're like a straggle of cattle
tamed from savanna ruminants
chewing the cud from buds on the family tree.

                Browse along the hominid highway,

stumble and   evolve
towards magneto, lit   technological
fields, where all the bovines die.

Huddle Besieged

a grave marker for your postulate.
Your time's iterative, a sequence, sucking its ancestral
tail, curves to corruption, crawls into a wise man's
skull and counts. Evolves—a gentler ape
making kinder use of aeons diluted into time,
shattered, re-constructed into goals truly sapient.

Lucy Spurns Bondage

You are a Paleoanthropologist—
a word flailed by its eight syllables.

A serf, paying his fief
to unearth my fossil.

Submit to species exceptionalism
and post-colonial regimes—
the maculate iris wipes itself clean

of

Africa's famine corpses,

                      their bones too fresh to fossilise.

You're in bondage to these people

who like to label others
long deceased in memory.

You sneer, mired in
the politics of

nationalism and dread.

They store my bones like
sword shards in a safe

in Addis Ababa

while millions
infect and starve and die.

All so man can polish his
geode ego.

Free me of your trap
when naming me:

southern ape from Africa.
Free me and scribe your

species obituary
Carve it in stone or distil

your mistakes, to acid-etch in symbols
a future can read of the folly in your epithets.

Lucy on History's Bones

He transgressed
and flung my bones to the stars
along with his fire's ashes
to ignite the Milky Way.
So I left him. My footprints
wind-wiped from Hadar's grey sand.

I wander the world,
a celestial being,
searching for a dwelling
in an animal guise.
The evening campfire ashes
glisten in the night sky.
The light will guide me home.

Lucy's Glitz

Why
am
I
fondling cut
cellophane flowers,
rustling
in pastel
shades
of sunflower and green,
petals
and pistils awry?

I can have blue diamonds,
compressed as my bones
polished,
               cut
into wealth and power, as tainted of man's rapacity,
as of earth's geologic past

they lustre and last.

Instead, I got glitz.
He got research grants.

Lucy's a Debutante

Can I resist a dictator's
embrace? I am bone, but
my stony heart does not absorb
the suffering of a people I've never met.

The man who names me in Africa,
Director General
of Ethiopia's Ministry of Culture
calls me Dinkinesh,
to mean I was marvellous.

To astonish oppressed humanity?
Or compressed in my bones
a plea for his economic necessity?

I'm a hit,
a debutante in Addis Ababa,
resplendently laid for the world's media—
my coming out party, my presentation at court
if you like—
after three million years looking
for my 'Deb's delight,'
eligible for his possession.

On a planet where everyone wants a glimpse,
here's Lucy.
In the home that claimed me,
famine strides,
an emperor is strangled.
A junta rules.
Nothing to disturb my diamond fame.

Lucy's Diamond Debut

It was the glitter of a diamond,
star-dusted, the night he found me
blown on the marketing wind
that saw me appear in crosswords,
cartoons, on African Red Bush tea,
in coffee shops, a fruit juice bar,
and political magazines.
His sole control in Ethiopia's Afar
drinking beer in the Lussy Bar.

The Knee Joint

In all the beer joints
in all the world, the Lussy Bar's
a shanty desert dive.

He sits cradling his first knee joint,
lounging, his elbows slopping
in the counter's spilled beer.

A rummage
in a local burial mound
for a sapient comparison

telling him I was bipedal.
Grave robbing aside,
confirmation found.

I stride from my burial mound,
scanning the horizon for hamburger joints.
Addis Ababa and stardom bound.

Lucy Doin' the Loco-Motion

and sayin' hi to Kylie Minogue

informative sample of hominin fossils older than 3.0 Ma. *Studies on* subjects ranging from the rise of *striding bipedal locomotion* to the origin of the *uniquely human* pattern of growth and development to the evolution of hominin dietary adaptations have *drawn* heavily *on* data from the remains of A. afarensis. Taxonomic and phylo genetic research, which experienced *a major renaissance* in palaeoanthropology *beginning* around the time when *A*. afarensis was discovered, has benefited from the extensive baseline data on fossil hominin skeletal and dental variation residing in the Hadar site-sample. Some of the research topics that focus on A. afarensis—the extent to which terrestrial bipedality was the committed form of locomotion, the *degree of sexual* dimorphism in body size and implications for *social behavior, and the* "*shape*" of the phylogenetic tree prior to the emergence *of* the *Homo* and robust australopith lineages, to name just three prominent examples—are still *actively debated* today, which merely *drives home the message* that finding solutions to scientific problems in palaeoanthropology is not just a function *of* augmenting fossil sample size (or even of the completeness of remains: witness the central role of the *"Lucy"* skeleton *in the locomotion debate*).

Lucy Reflects on Fame

It's hard
to become a fossil.
it cost me a lot—my life.
Life has a taste
for a nut hardened corpse
with no kernel.

Few of us get eroded
and recycled, cut
from shale or schist
and immortalised
in rock
of longevity—
those that do skull-grin.

Perpetuity and cursed
celebrity?
That's how I became Lucy
each bone laid bare
precisely on my tar-black
museum bed.

I'll colour to a cashew.

Lucy Worshipped

He hears Mohamed mutter
as the Afar stand in prayer
in a scorching
sulphurous sandy hollow.

Mohamed says:

She was found in Hadar;
as an Afar.
So, all humans on earth
today descend to them

through Lucy.

    This makes me wince as I clamber
    back in my museum cupboard.

    Did I die, an echo, worshipped after an aeon?
    Dug up in the Afar triangle, not as an Afar.
    No responsibility for my bones to shoulder.

His embarrassing reply, an unscientific:

That makes me happy.

    I rage:

I'm no theory
    you stamp on my nature.
    I was/am my simple self
long ago beside a river.

Lucy's Exile

In exile, having my matrix removed
he never left me alone,
preparing me
for publication
and return home.

When my fame faded, he takes
me back to an arid land,
tucked in his holdall,
with his worries about crashing
and losing me on his mind.

Back to a dictator.

Later he comes after me
lusting for
better Lucys,
in his mind's eye, digging the motherlode
of his origins.

Does he express his disgust at the
predatory violence of his world?

I would prefer to face a sabre tooth
from my youth than tyrants, who strangle
and let millions starve . . .

I could pluck food from the tree's embrace.

Dinkinesh

Am I a 'missing link'?
I'd rather go 'apeshit,'
than my identity
harnessed to his group.

He chipped me from a cloak of rock,
sculpting an identity
as a cheerleader for man's evolution—
a woman to shake the apple from man's family tree.

I'm called Lucy.
Named for a popular song,
unable to defend
my honour when I fossilised

into an Ethiopian swelter, baked in the oven
of tribal law and tradition,
firing the burden of a country's pride,
for a land I never lived in.

He dug me up, then I'm claimed
by a politician who listened
to my excavator and said:
You know, she is an Ethiopian.
She needs an Ethiopian name.

Yes! He agreed, relieved.
Worried to cause offence
with an image of an English girl
under Marmalade skies.

What do you suggest? he stuttered.

Dinkinesh is the name for her.
In Amharic meaning
I'm something marvellous, of us.

In a land once greened, today drought and sand
humanity was born, they say—
though they didn't state it in those terms.

They needed the distraction of my name—
this was taken as read, man-to-man.

I felt claws of competing claims
pricking my bones.

Join Me in Deep Time

ivory skulled sapiens.
I'll fondle your rock remains, proposition
shamans, cast your teeth as dice, divine games of time,
for societies in monkey planet ancestry;
commit mistakes, imperfect ape,
in miasma of wise man.

Lucy as Lucifer

I despair at the men who scuffle
my bones
and lick them clean of meaning,

as they gnaw
and worry the forty-seven
remaining bits of my body.

I even lost my Lux to
Lucifer.

As two men decided after
obstetric analysis
of my fragmented skeleton,

that I was male.
No consent.
Just a snuffle at my remains

renamed me
for the
son of the morning.

My discoverer's defense,
since he found me,

is that I was small for my age
and best interpreted as a female
of the species.

The wolf-pack alpha's
last growl.

Lucy and Lucifer

Why seek to rename me as a fallen angel?
Why Lucifer, why not Larry or Lou?
What was their angle?

Well, both derive from the light.
The transcendent one.
The fallen one.

You're Capering Urban Grasslands

along with the other apes.
Slashed by a scythe's steel edge, cut slivers of time
into parings of progress, propositional.
Struggle in parching dust, no three wise-men
to lead in petroleum deserts, late sapiens.
Invite ruin in necropsy of your ancestry.

Lucy and the Neanderthal

Lucy purrs to the lumpy
browed skull ahead
in the fossil queue:

*You, Neanderthal
I'm extinct like you,
so we can't be close.
We may not be ultimately
related, you know, though
we share a museum shelf.*

*I'll come up the stony epochs
and see you in due course.
For you, I'll make an exception
and snog outside my species.*

Peking Man

as Homo erectus user of fire, they say.
His bones exposed in 1920s China,
then misplaced in the fires of a world at war
by soldiers, who buried them
when the Japanese invaded.
Then dug up again by retreating
American troops when Mao took over
in savage revolution.

Re-buried in footlockers
under a Chinese parking lot,
they say.

Poor Peking man,
colonially mis-named for a Beijing
of a time to come/past.
Dug from Dragon Bone Hill.
Then lost.
His bones once
used as a machine gun rest, still
never a rest for adulation
like mine as I recline in
my Addis Ababa Museum.

Peking man deprived.
Never a re-constructed 'person' like me.
Losing an opportunity for a name, and the fame.

Homo Ergaster

Homo ergaster's,   preserved cranium
I almost knew her
she went to a future,   to an   US.

Sockets were her eyes after the moulder.
Patina-ed surface—geological accretions
double-arched brow-ridge.

Polished brown   gothic   quizzical.
Millenia churning rock,
residing in stone beside Lake Turkana
till found,   till collected.

Mrs Ples Provokes Hominid Fever

Maybe I was lucky
my discoverer
was   gentle
caressing me with his brushes
         other bone hunters   brutal
searching for their hominid past
         blasting breccia
cracking skulls in search
finding Mrs Ples   dainty/sweet   little woman
later speculated to be a man
            she
barely survived her skull
in two fragments   lacking teeth
with her crystal-lined brain cavity
naked/exposed and on show
her dehydrated cavalier
scrabbling South African dust
where spirits told him to look
concluding she was a
            small brained man like being
. . . very nearly human
this human
chasing his horizon for posterity
his discoveries, telling a story
                  of progress
when he'd written the story   he put down the pen
and whispered   *Now that's finished . . . and so am I*
before drying into parch-boned sand

Who's on Lucy's Team?

Sixty millennia huddling a planet
recreant. Our anthropological gambol
means kicking balls, we're barely
constituent as sapient, relegating
other teams.

Team Neanderthal, Denisovans,
Naledi, Floresiensis—surviving as
legend. We fucked some, mingling our
heredity, where ghost populations, lurk
unmentioned;

our genes fester species yet to
identify. So, I gaze at Lucy contemplating,
hidden in paleoanthropology,
fragments, Adam's rib
remaining.

She never played for us, distant in
season consigned to oblivion.

Look Up Man

strip-stone your predecessor,
Lucy—an ancient hominid
in harmony with rock, not Homo sapiens.
Time speaks bitter words: you frittered time
intoning a rook's caw—tardy wise man!
Count time to avoid future's propositions.

Prediction

For I see an ancient simian
evolve into a viral species. Isolation—
fracturing threats with love—from the margin,
generation by lost generation.
Panic purchase—a plastic bag's provision
then Skype yourself to speciation.
New Homo from snake tongued sapiens.
Arise, a new species, your technology
evolved into your skulls, limpets to your psyche
for hundreds of thousands of isolate years arise:

Homo capitalistsensis,
Homo computerensis,
Homo mobileensis,
Homo pandemicensis.

Go forth, take census

populate a cosmos. I'll re-fossilize,
mothballed in a museum cabinet.

Lucy Laid Out

My bones laid out on indigo cloth
as medieval sword splinters,
in a cultural annexation.
Weathered the shade of walnut kernels.
Forty-seven pieces, much of me
never found. Laid schematically,
anatomically where they were in my life.
As my lineage, heading to celebrate
my obscured humanity. I'm Lucy, for lux—light
raising the intensity on life.
Regimented ribs in an arch beside
the lined vertebrae of my backbone
as he re-arranges me. Shattered pelvis
shaped like my heart not for him,
from the girl with sun in her eyes.
My mandible's there, no longer
masticating lumps of life.
It's placed with care like a prominent smile
under my five found skull slivers.
I know nothing of the scientific method
observation, evaluation, hypothesis
that identified me as afarensis.
I rest in conceit, my bones serving notice
through populous aeons—he may be lost.
Sadly, I'm no guide or shaman
laid out for funerary-wedding,
absent for his divination.

Advance to Dim Futures

disregard your span
as a self-infected species—you're no wise man,
for descendants no responsible ancestor.
Possess your ironic name as sapiens,
rarely rational in sapient propositions;
after all you're only a cleverer ape.

Lucy Grieves

I eroded out of the rock in Afar
in endless sand and punishing heat. I've
been stunned to my stony end, never a star.
For aeons I lay, missing the revive.

Hippo's roar echoes epochal reset,
while a Deinotherium roots leafage
into its gaping mouth. Fig tree's night nest,
the cool freshet, my thirst to assuage.

Rustling leaves cloaking me as if a wraith.
Smooth reptilian boughs, Eden's snake-like ilex.
Cradling baby's fur, as I fall to earth.
I would cut this tree today with an axe.

I'd fashion a wardrobe, my bare hands alone,
to hang a swish fur coat off my backbone.

The Sediments of Time

I address Meave Leakey (over eras not distance)

Meave, as you sift sediments of time
through your ageing fingers,
are they stabbed uncomfortably
by the shards and fragments of bone
you never finished assembling?

Sieve fossil beds for skeletal meaning
in genus and kindred demise.
With the playfulness of nurturing,
bigger pictures subsume facets
of your care and compassion.

Re-constructing skulls by the Turkana
as your baby, feet in cool water, played
and a hippo splashed in the lake.

With grace you and your team
read the rocks, reconstructing habitats
of the fossils you find.

In my wonder
as I leave earth at last,
with your gentle touch
your kinder reading of my bones,
would I stay and keep my name?

Lucy Fossilised Past-Future

It's like trying to appease a little god.
—David Farrie, *Footprints: In Search of Future Fossils*

I

Excreting on your patch
is a snag if your excrement
is unsafe for thousands of years
so scoop the poop
and sly to bury it
to make it someone else's problem
or
        tell bacteria where the deed was done

write a message into the DNA
of this long-lived god of basics
in a cypher
        you gamble
                the future can figure out
so that future can avoid the eroded place
where the past festers till it's safe

II

Violate a life
I shared a world with
        as if to write a sonnet
        in bacterial innards
in a prayer to these tiny gods
that you existed   that you mattered
hoping the cells will pause
in millions of years of continuance
to write a placatory sonnet back

III

Sear my message on the code of a life
that has no interest in your
hubristic burdens   scaring and crushing
their life-generation   the germs do not
comprehend or even wish to understand
what you have to say

IV

My discoverer's familiar
with fossilised scat
so long as it doesn't glow
And he can prod
it for its messages from the past
My minor god
will take me back to the Awash
river near where we all first met
and wash
away a species' stench   in it

I'm Lucy, No Wise Man

I precede sapiens
a hominid, a gentler proposition
I crouch
with your ancestors where aeons consume fruit
at Omega's edge.

Entombed

too late to etch a message on my
stone-bones that your species left dark,
deadly artefacts and thoughts; exhume
these errors for a deep future to avoid.

Becoming Like Lucy

and like can turn to love in the joining . . .

Fantasy of my skull sans rotted flesh   dire circumstance on
my demise   dead on oozed riverbed   dead sun
darkens to rain   flash floods submerge and bathe my
corpse for the task ahead   Bones scattered   then scavenged

Un-biased—my

skull settled in watery hole   turning to sedimentary stone
molecule by measured molecule   all shred of identity
gone   Impressions left in earth's matrix
Bathed in mineral rich
water until   when the years have counted

indeterminate

I'm rock   like Lucy
I'm rock   fossilised surprisingly fast

What the fate of my dentures? Does plastic petrify beneath the
flint?

Or eaten by minerals   tectonically   shattered blasted then
mined

denatured

Notes

This collection explores the objectification of long-dead individuals through two characters. Both of the characters are imaginative creations with some basis in fact.

One source of my fascination is a book co-authored by Donald Johanson called *From Lucy to Language*. This book labels and catalogues the fossilized remains of distant hominid ancestors. Its attraction to me is its carefully lit photography. These images of ivory shaded perfections, shards of ancient individuals, captivated the artist within me.

Lucy is a counterpoint to the scientific lust for collecting data. This need for information that is structured into a 'database' of our ancestry, where we showcase these relics. They become species representatives, finding their resting place as branches on the family tree of Homo sapiens exceptionalism. She is an argument for extending her humanity on her terms. Lucy was/is a living being.

"The Naming of Fossils": The reference to Old Possum is to the source of this poem as a parody of The Naming of Cats, in T.S. Eliot's *Old Possum's Book of Practical Cats*. Old Possum is a nickname bestowed upon Eliot by friends and colleagues.

"Lucy on History's Bones": Hadar is the name of the site where Lucy's remains were found and is part of the Afar region of Ethiopia.

"Lucy's Diamond Debut": This poem is based on an event described in Johanson's *Lucy's Legacy: The Quest for Human Origins*.

"The Knee Joint": The 'grave robbing' is extrapolated from an incident in *Lucy—the Beginnings of Humankind* by Johanson and Maitland A. Edey.

"Lucy Doin' the Loco-Motion": The academic text used in this poem is copied from the paper "'Lucy' Redux: A Review of Research on Australopithecus afarensis," William H. Kimbel and Lucas K. Delezene Institute of Human Origins, School of Human Evolution and Social Change, Arizona State University.

"Lucy's Exile": The matrix is the enclosing mass of rock surrounding the fossil. Paleoanthropologists talk of days of patient work with a microscope and air drill, sometimes taking years to remove the embedded fossil.

"Dinkinesh": The surreal Beatle's song from the 1960s "Lucy in the Sky with Diamonds" was playing on a tape deck in the background as Johanson and his team celebrated his lucky find. Her Ethiopian name is less well known.

"The Sediments of Time": Meave Leakey's autobiography lends its title to this poem. This poem is a tribute to Meave who is from a family of paleoanthropologists who had some disagreements with Lucy's rediscoverer. Meave has an analytical but respectful approach to her profession in her book, seeming, to me anyway, to be at odds with a more aggressive and competitive approach among other scientists. I interpret this as a deep respect for Lucy and her kin in a way which I hope Lucy would approve of.

"Lucy Fossilised Past-Future": The poet Christian Bök tried to write a sonnet into the code of life.
poetryfoundation.org/harriet-books/2011/04/the-xenotext-works

About the Author

John Moody lives in Scotland. He has published in *Dawntreader, Dreich, The SquawkBack, PocketPoetry, Southlight, Steel Jackdaw, Aayo Magazine,* and *Lazuli Literary Group,* and in anthologies from Pure Slush Books and Coin-Operated Press. *I Am Loud Productions* has published videos of his readings. He has been shortlisted for the Mirrorball Clydebuilt Poetry apprenticeship.

www.ingramcontent.com/pod-product-compliance
Lightning Source LLC
Chambersburg PA
CBHW071013160426
43193CB00012B/2032